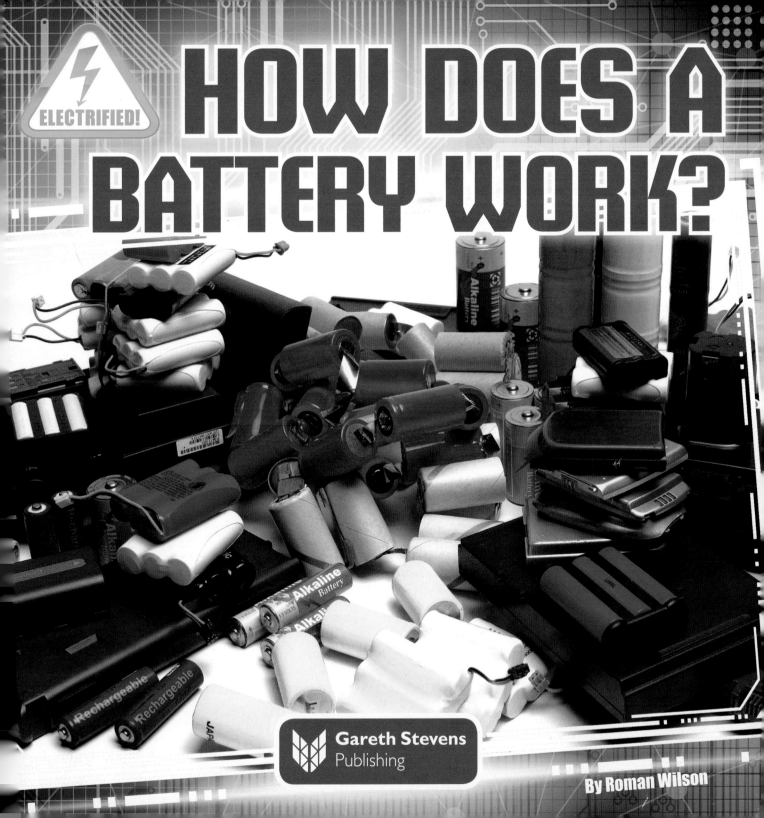

ELECTRIFIED!

HOW DOES A BATTERY WORK?

Gareth Stevens
Publishing

By Roman Wilson

Please visit our website, www.garethstevens.com. For a free color catalog of all our high-quality books, call toll free 1-800-542-2595 or fax 1-877-542-2596.

Library of Congress Cataloging-in-Publication Data

Wilson, Roman.
  How does a battery work? / Roman Wilson.
      pages cm. — (Electrified!)
  Includes bibliographical references and index.
  ISBN 978-1-4339-8400-6 (pbk.)
  ISBN 978-1-4339-8401-3 (6-pack)
  ISBN 978-1-4339-8399-3 (library binding)
  1. Electric batteries—Juvenile literature. 2. Electricity—Juvenile literature. 3. Electric circuit—Juvenile literature. I. Title.
  TK2901.W55 2013
  621.31'2424—dc23

                                    2012020694

First Edition

Published in 2013 by
Gareth Stevens Publishing
111 East 14th Street, Suite 349
New York, NY 10003

Copyright © 2013 Gareth Stevens Publishing

Designer: Katelyn E. Reynolds
Editor: Therese Shea

Photo credits: Cover, p. 1 Don Farrall/Photodisc/Getty Images; cover, p. 1 (logo) iStockphoto/Thinkstock.com; cover, pp. 1, 3–24 (background) Lukas Radavicius/Shutterstock.com; cover, pp. 1, 3–24 (image frame) VikaSuh/Shutterstock.com; p. 5 Rayes/Photodisc/Thinkstock.com; p. 7 Charles D. Winters/Photo Researchers/Getty Images; p. 9 Hemera/Thinkstock.com; p. 11 Zoonar/Thinkstock.com; p. 13 nikkytok/Shutterstock.com; p. 15 Encyclopaedia Britannica/Universal Images Group/Getty Images; p. 17 Smileus/Shutterstock.com; p. 19 SSPL/Getty Images; p. 21 Universal Images Group via Getty Images.

Printed in the United States of America

CPSIA compliance information: Batch #CW13GS: For further information contact Gareth Stevens, New York, New York at 1-800-542-2595.

CONTENTS

Words in the glossary appear in **bold** type the first time they are used in the text.

BATTERY POWER!

How many things can you think of that use batteries? Probably quite a few. Watches, MP3 players, computers, cell phones, and cars are just a few battery-powered **devices**. Now imagine that, instead of batteries, you needed to plug them in every time you used them. Your car wouldn't get too far!

Luckily, battery power allows us to move around freely. Did you ever wonder how a battery works and where its **energy** comes from? Read on to find out!

Without batteries, you'd have to be near an electrical outlet just to listen to a song or play a handheld video game.

CHEMICAL ENERGY

Electrical energy, or electricity, isn't created. It's **converted** from another kind of energy. Batteries store **chemicals** and turn chemical energy into electrical energy.

A circuit is a path of electricity that begins and ends at the same point. When a battery is connected to a circuit, it's the beginning and ending point. The battery pushes electricity into the circuit. As the electricity travels throughout the device, it gives the device power. When you remove the battery, the circuit is broken and electricity stops flowing.

POWER FACT!

Off switches are another way to stop the energy flow in a circuit. Batteries still lose a bit of chemical energy in devices switched to "off," though.

Batteries can look very different, but all use chemicals to make electricity.

WHAT'S IN THE CHEMICALS?

Chemicals in batteries—and all matter—are made up of **atoms**. Atoms are made up of tiny **particles** called protons, neutrons, and electrons. Protons and neutrons form the atom's **core**, and electrons circle the core.

Electrons and protons have a property called an electric charge. Electrons have a negative charge. Protons have a positive charge. Neutrons have no overall charge.

Like charges push away, or repel, each other. Unlike charges draw, or attract, each other. The protons in an atom's core attract the circling electrons.

Usually, an atom has the same number of protons and electrons. The positive and negative charges are balanced.

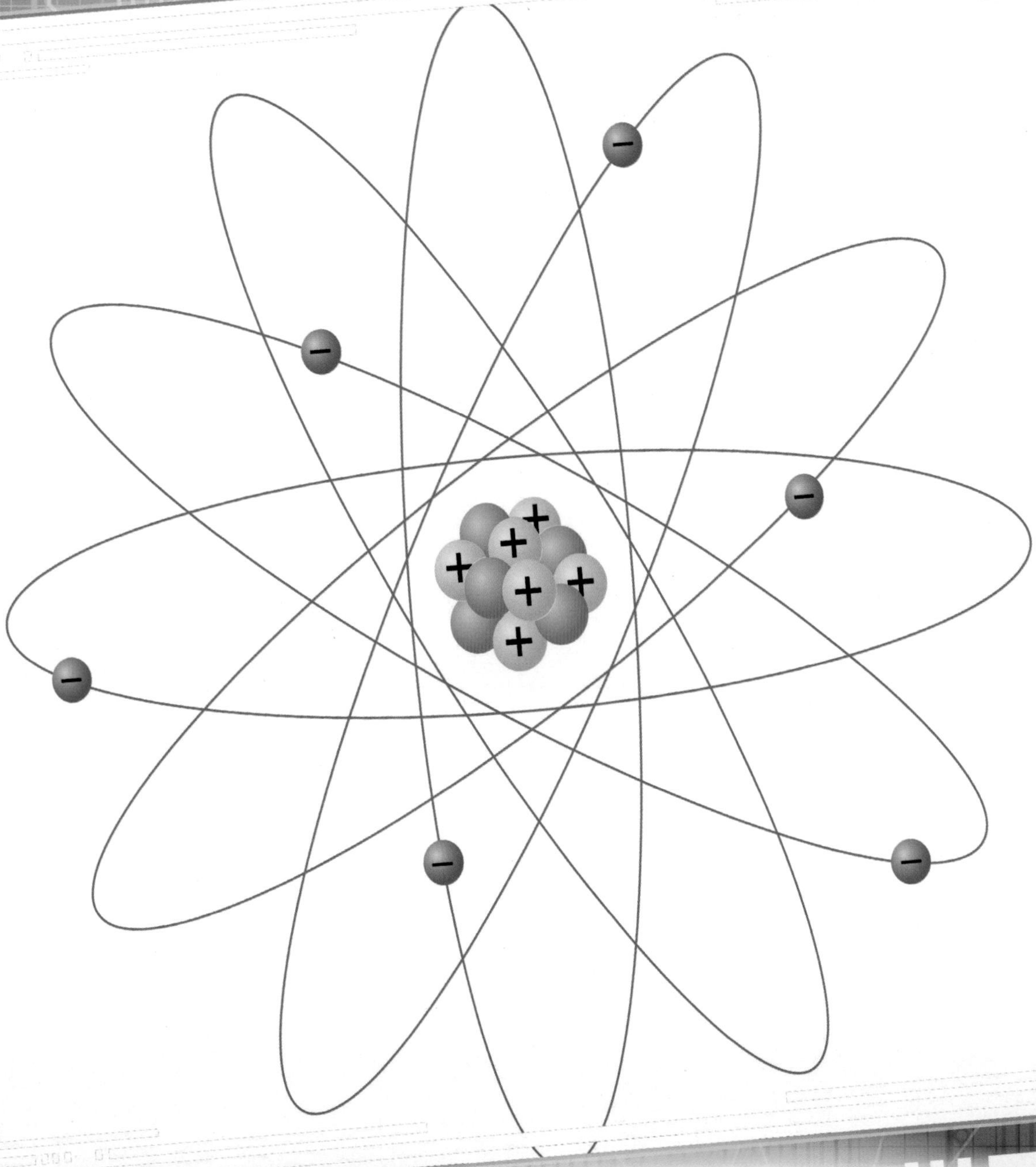

ELECTRODES

Batteries have two **terminals** on the outside. One may be marked with a negative sign (–) and the other with a positive sign (+). In 9-volt batteries, these terminals are side by side. In AA, C, and some other batteries, the terminals are located at opposite ends.

Inside the battery, the terminals are connected to **electrodes**. The negative electrode is called the anode. The positive electrode is the cathode. Each of these electrodes is responsible for a chemical reaction that creates a flow of electricity.

The outside of the battery is usually made of metal or plastic.

ELECTROLYTES

Batteries contain one or more parts called cells. The cells hold a chemical mixture called an electrolyte. The electrolyte works with the electrodes to produce chemical reactions.

The chemical reaction at a battery's anode separates electrons from their atoms. As the electrons build up, they escape the negatively charged area. They're attracted to the cathode. However, the electrolyte won't allow them to pass through it. The electrons must move to the cathode by going around the circuit.

POWER FACT!

An electrolyte may be a liquid or a dry paste.

Low Battery

COMPLETING THE CIRCUIT

The free electrons moving through the circuit make up the flow of electricity, also called the current. As they flow, they supply the circuit—and the device—with electrical power.

When electrons reach the cathode, another chemical reaction takes place. The electrons attach to atoms there and reenter the battery. The circuit continues.

Atoms that have gained or lost electrons are called ions. Batteries depend on atoms becoming ions to create electricity. Another one of the electrolyte's jobs is to carry ions inside the battery.

POWER FACT!

As the battery repels and attracts electrons, the chemicals within it begin to change into other chemicals. This is why the chemical reactions stop working after a time and a battery "dies."

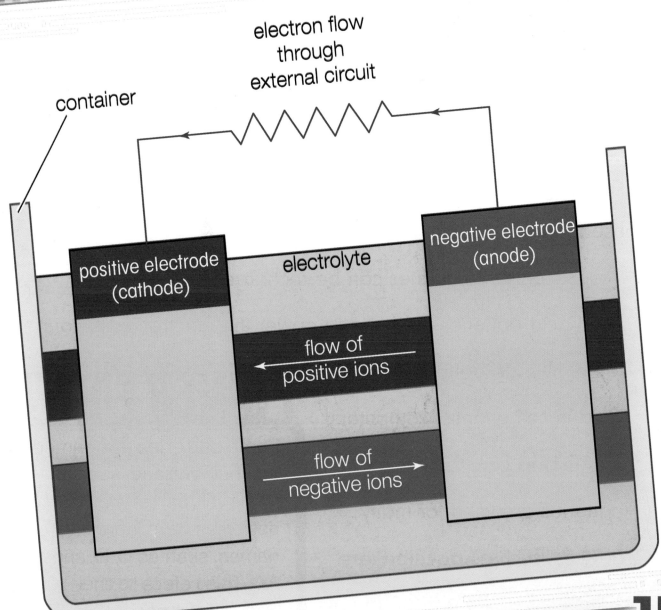

electron flow
through
external circuit

container

positive electrode
(cathode)

electrolyte

negative electrode
(anode)

flow of
positive ions

flow of
negative ions

KINDS OF BATTERIES

There are two groups of batteries: primary and secondary. Primary, or single use, batteries cannot be recharged. Once the chemical energy runs out in the battery, it can't be used again. Alkaline and carbon–zinc batteries are primary batteries used to power small devices.

Secondary batteries can be recharged by electricity. Lead-acid batteries are used to power the electronics in cars. Metal hydride batteries are used in cell phones, computers, and **hybrid** cars. Lithium-ion batteries are used for many devices, such as **pacemakers**!

POWER FACT!

Some batteries are named for their **voltage**, such as the 9-volt battery. Other batteries have letter names, such as C, D, and AA. This refers to their size, not voltage.

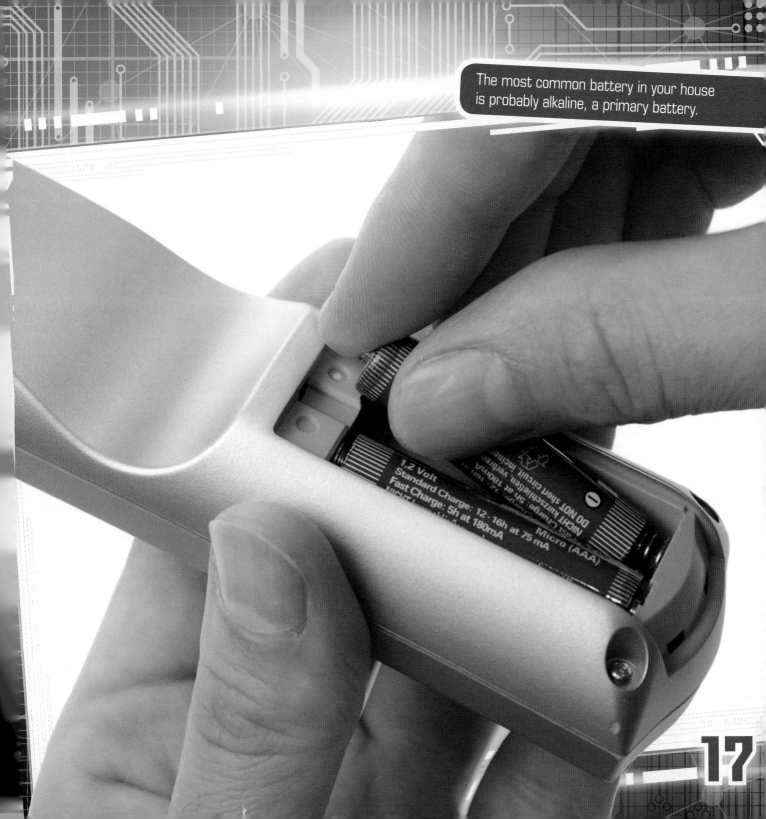

1.2 Volt
Standard Charge: 12-16h at 180mA
Fast Charge: 5h at 180mA
Fast Charge: 5h at 75 mA
Micro (AAA)

A SHORT HISTORY

Italian scientist Count Alessandro Volta first discovered that chemicals could be used to make an electrical charge in 1799. He created a battery out of metal plates separated by saltwater-soaked paper and cardboard. This battery was called the voltaic pile.

In the 1830s, British scientist Michael Faraday showed how chemical reactions push an electrical current along in a battery. In 1836, John Daniell, another British scientist, introduced a battery that used copper and zinc. In 1896, the first batteries sold to the public were called Columbia dry cells.

POWER FACT!

Scientists found clay jars in what is now Iraq that may have worked somewhat like batteries. The jars date back to around 250 BC.

The voltaic pile looked like this. It was the first device to provide a steady supply of electricity.

RECYCLE IT!

We know we should recycle cans and paper, but did you know you should recycle batteries? Even secondary batteries die after a time. When they do, don't throw them in the trash. They contain materials that can be recycled. In fact, batteries contain metals that shouldn't be mixed in with other trash. The metals can do harm if they leak out.

In 2010, the program Call2Recycle collected 6.7 million pounds (3.04 million kg) of batteries. Check with your local government to see if it has a special recycling program for batteries.

POWER FACT!

Americans buy nearly 3 billion primary batteries every year to power radios, toys, cell phones, watches, computers, and power tools.

Battery-recycling centers like this one break down batteries into chemicals and parts that can be used for other products.

GLOSSARY

atom: one of the smallest bits of matter

chemical: matter that can be mixed with other matter to cause changes

convert: to cause to change form

core: the central part of something

device: a tool or machine made to perform a task

electrode: matter through which electricity enters or leaves a circuit

energy: power used to do work

hybrid: able to run on electricity and gasoline but using one or the other at a time

pacemaker: a battery-operated device placed in the body to keep the heart beating regularly

particle: a very small piece of something

terminal: a point on a battery where electricity enters or leaves a circuit

voltage: a measurement of electrical energy

FOR MORE INFORMATION

Books

Oxlade, Chris. *Using Batteries*. Chicago, IL: Heinemann Library, 2012.

Richardson, Adele. *Electricity: A Question and Answer Book*. Mankato, MN: Capstone Press, 2006.

Young, Karen Romano. *Junkyard Science: 20 Projects and Experiments About Junk, Garbage, Waste, Things We Don't Need Anymore, and Ways to Recycle or Reuse It—or Lose It*. Washington, DC: National Geographic, 2010.

Websites

How Batteries Work
electronics.howstuffworks.com/everyday-tech/battery.htm
Find out more about the history of batteries and how they power our devices.

Lemon Battery
pbskids.org/zoom/activities/sci/lemonbattery.html
Learn how to make a battery using lemons!

INDEX